CROWN *Her*
DIAMOND
REMEMBERING YOU ARE A DAUGHTER OF A KING

ADRIENNE L. FIGURES

Copyright © 2020 by Adrienne L. Figures
All rights reserved. This book or any portion thereof may not be reproduced or used in any manner whatsoever without the express written permission of the publisher except for the use of brief quotations in a book review.

Limits of Liability and Disclaimer of Warranty
The author and publisher shall not be liable for your misuse of this material. This book is strictly for informational purposes. The purpose of this book is to educate and entertain. The author and publisher do not guarantee anyone following these techniques, suggestions, tips, ideas, or strategies will become successful. The author and publisher shall have neither liability nor responsibility to anyone with respect to any loss or damage caused, or alleged to be caused, directly or indirectly by the information contained in this book. Views expressed in this publication do not necessarily reflect the views of the publisher.

Printed in the United States of America

Keen Vision Publishing, LLC
www.keen-vision.com
ISBN: 978-1-948270-59-5

What every **WOMAN** *should know about*

DIAMONDS

DIAMONDS *are created under pressure deep within the Earth's crust.*

Miners have to dig and chisel DIAMONDS *out of dirt and rocks.*

Before DIAMONDS *are used, they endure a rough process of being cleaned, shaped, and cut.*

The crown of DIAMONDS *include a* **table** *(the flat top of it) and* **facets** *(the cuts that make a* DIAMOND *shine.)*

The more a DIAMOND *has been cut...the more beautiful it will be.*

Every DIAMOND *is unique.*

CONTENTS

TABLE TALK	7
FACET 1: Love Yourself, Girl!	13
FACET 2: Mirror, Mirror On the Wall	19
FACET 3: Positivity is Key	25
FACET 4: Sis. Stop Comparing	29
FACET 5: Support Your Sister	35
FACET 6: Let That Grudge Go, Girl!	41
FACET 7: Manage Your Emotions Well	47
FACET 8: A Mother's Love	53
FACET 9: But God	61
FACET 10: Just Be Free	67
FACET 11: Well-Fed or Well-Nourished	73
FACET 12: Find Your Fire, Boo	79
FACET 13: Gospel Carrier or Gossip Carrier	85
FACET 14: Standards & Boundaries	89
FACET 15: Your Cookies	97
FACET 16: Microwaved Situationships	103
FACET 17: Your Now vs God's Not Yet	107
FACET 18: Your Prayer Life	113
FACET 19: A Woman of Faith	119

FACET 20: Encourage Others	125
FACET 21: You're A Wild Woman	129
Words From the Author	133
Dedication	135
About the Author	137
Stay Connected	139

TABLE TALK

My heart goes out to women all around the world. I'm concerned about how we value ourselves, or should I say, the lack of valuing ourselves. You're probably looking at me side-eyed like, "What do you mean?" Day after day, I watch as women accept, tolerate and deal with anything. Many have not been taught the do's and don'ts of being a woman. They are unaware of how to adapt to different environments and ignorant of how to carry themselves as women. Many of us didn't have women in our lives who kept it 100.

Personally, I had women present who helped raised me, but I required a different type of handling. I needed the women who loved me to tell me like it was and not spare my feelings. I needed tough love. I wish they had sat me down and taught me how to love myself properly. I wish I had learned not to be more consumed with waiting for my Boaz than I was with preparing for him and allowing God to work in me. Also, I missed lessons about celebrating other women as I built my legacy. As a result, I dealt with a lot of bull crap and wasn't true to myself.

Let's face it. Many of us didn't get the tools we needed growing up. We often fantasize about conversations that should have taken place. We say things like, "Well, if someone had told me how to be a lady, then I would not have gotten into a lot of the mess I got into." The truth of the matter is, those who reared us, did the best they could. They taught us what they knew. Once we realize what's missing, it's on us to gain the mentors and insight we need to improve ourselves. And that's what this book is all about.

Sis, can we be real for a moment? If the information you're about to read is going to help you, you've got to listen! Sometimes, we get advice and do the complete opposite. Personally, some of the women I hung around tried to tell me how to handle certain situations, but I was very hardheaded and wouldn't listen. I thought I needed to bump my head and make my own decisions. If I had listened to the people who tried to warn me about certain things, I probably could have avoided heartbreaks, mess-ups, teenage pregnancy, and living out of control. I would not have given my cookie out to all the taste testers I was attracted to.

On the flip side, because I was hardheaded and went through so much at a young age, I gained a lot of insight about life. We've all made mistakes. However, if we look at them through the right lense, our mistakes qualify us to help others prevent the same pitfalls. This book is the fruit of my decision to allow others to glean from my mistakes instead of hiding behind them.

For many years, I was ashamed of who I am. I felt like I was too loud for this person, too direct for that person, a little too hood for this one, and way too churchy for the other. After a while, maintaining different personalities became draining and confusing. I didn't know what people wanted from me. Oh, but once I began to love myself, all of those personalities went out of the window. I was like, "Forget all of that people-pleasing! I am going to be me regardless of who doesn't like it." I have learned that there will be people who will not like me based on my looks, boldness, or personality. I no longer apologize for who God has created me to be, the mistakes I've made, and where I come from. When people seem not to like me, I just pray that they will find their dopeness and the confidence to rock it too!

I created this book to help women all over the world learn to love themselves, and others like Christ loves us. This book is for the woman who never had big sisters, aunties, or a mother to sit them down and keep it real with them. This book is for the teenager who doesn't listen because she feels like no one truly understands. This book is for the young girl who has made mistakes and is ready to turn a new leaf but doesn't know how. This book is for those who wish they had a circle of girlfriends to tell them the brutal, but honest truth. Ladies. This book is for all of us! I want us to see our value instead of expecting the world to validate our worth. I want us to look in the mirror and, regardless of what we've been through, love the person staring back at you!

When God gave me the title, Crown Her Diamond, I didn't really understand what it meant. I did some research, and I found out that diamonds aren't found the same way we see them in the store. Diamonds are pulled out of dirt, rock, and stone deep within the earth. Despite how valuable they are, they still require a little work before they are put on display. The crown of a diamond is what makes the diamond shine, glow, and sparkle. The crown of a diamond consists of several cuts or facets. The more facets a diamond has, the more it will reflect light. Like a diamond, I was once very rough and raw. However, once I submitted to God's process, (His cutting, cleaning, and shaping), I became the beautiful woman He created me to be. You see, we all are like precious diamonds that have to go through a process to shine bright. I'm just here to help you along your journey.

In this book, I will be completely transparent, honest, and totally ME! I will share stories that I've never shared with those close to me. Why? Because you've heard enough "pretty stories." Also, you'll find opportunities to self-reflect and interact with what you read. Be sure to intentionally answer each question. You can write your responses in this book, or in your journal. My prayer is that as I reveal the wisdom I learned in my most difficult seasons, you will be able to see yourself and know that you are not alone. Hopefully, you will be able to see that your past does not disqualify you from love and being able to love and value yourself. I hope you find Crown Her Diamond very encouraging, inspiring, uplifting, but most importantly, REAL! So pull up a chair, sis. It's time for us to have a conversation or two.

FACET
One

"Love Yourself, Girl!"

Crown Her Diamond

Self-love is one of my favorite things to talk about! Love, love, and more love! (in my Uncle Luke voice.) But that hasn't always been my story! Let me ask you a question. Am I the only woman who did not love herself at all? I mean, I couldn't find a thing I loved about me. I remember when people would ask me my name, I would tell them, and when they responded, "Oh, that's beautiful," I would always answer with a rebuttal or brush their comments off. I remember the times I tried to change my middle name — because I didn't like it either. I believe it was because of the household I grew up in. Remember how Jenny in Forest Gump wanted God to make her a bird so she could fly far away? That was me! I wanted to go to some private island, change my name, and start completely over. Even though I knew that wasn't realistic, I was willing to do anything to get away. I had to realize that my life was designed for a purpose. The same goes for you, sis. No matter how bad things may seem, how much you don't like yourself, or how you wish you could change your life, everything about you is unique. You were created for a divine purpose. On your journey to understanding your purpose, you must also learn to love yourself.

The hate I had for myself was real! I hated the sound of my voice, my big smile, and my height. I hated that people considered me mean. The truth is, I only appeared mean to cover up my big heart and everything else I hated about myself. Here's the funny part. Even though I hated myself, I loved it when someone told me how beautiful I was. I know it's weird, but those compliments would blow my head up to the sky! One day, someone told me, "You can be Beyoncé fine, but have a bad attitude and still be ugly!" Baby, when I say that popped my little bubble! That's when I started to realize that I needed to make some changes.

    I had to start looking at why I despised certain characteristics and traits about myself. Once I dug deep, I began to address my self-hate and learn to love myself...every inch of me! Now, I love my height, and I know that someday, I'll meet someone who will be in love with these long legs. I love my BIG and gorgeous smile because it lights up a room on purpose. My voice isn't too deep; it just commands authority in situations. My heart is huge because I'm composed of lots of love. My blood doesn't look like everyone else's blood. I feel like I have little red hearts flowing through me filled with love! I learned to appreciate the things about myself that I didn't like and turned every negative thought about myself into a positive one. As a result, I stopped hiding behind a mean persona and learned how to be loving and kind to those around me. Do you see how that works? Sometimes, we place a lot of emphasis on loving others. While it is important to love others, it's impossible to do that when you don't love yourself. It's easier to love others when you are rooted in self-love. Wanna know the truth? Ya girl is still learning to love herself. It's a daily process, and it's not an easy task, my dear. I have some more growing to do, but as they say, "Rome was not built in a day!" So be patient with yourself. Don't rush the process — just enjoy the journey. Let's pray!

God,

    Thank you for your outpouring of love. Thank you for being the example of what love is supposed to look like. Your word says, "For God so loved the world that he gave his only begotten son that whoever believes in him should not perish but have everlasting life." John 3:16(NKJV). 1 John 4:8 (NKJV) says, "He who does not love does not know God, for God is love." As I learn to love myself, friends, family members, church members, and strangers, teach me how to love my enemies. Matthew 5:44-45 (NKJV) says, "But I say to you, love your enemies, bless those who curse you, and pray for those who spitefully use you and persecute you, that you may be sons of your Father in heaven." Thank you for your everlasting love. Fill me with the love this world and my future self need. It's in your name I pray. Amen!

What characteristics or traits about you do you dislike?

Let's think more positive about the things you listed above! How can you learn to love those parts of you?

FACET
Two

"Mirror, Mirror on the Wall...Who's the Dopest of Them All?"

Even though we shouldn't indulge in social media too much, sometimes, we can run across the most inspiring posts! I once saw a video of a little girl named Jayde. Her mother recorded her looking in the mirror, telling herself, "I'm Gorgeous!" It was the cutest thing I've ever seen. Even at a young age, Jayde teaches us a valuable lesson! We have to learn how to affirm the person we see in the mirror. Ladies, we are constantly on the go handling our business. Some of us are businesswomen, entrepreneurs, wives, mothers, daughters, sisters, nurses, and so forth. We always have to be somewhere and do something. While I totally understand, let me ask you a question, girlfriend. When is the last time you stopped, looked in the mirror, and told yourself how dope you are? You, my love, are GORGEOUS!

Let's take it a step further. While it's important to be confident about how we look, there's more to us than our pretty faces. When was the last time you affirmed what's beneath the surface? Has it been awhile? No worries. We are going to do a quick self-love exercise right now. Go to the nearest mirror. Stand there and look at yourself for five minutes. This is going to feel weird, but I want you to do it. Trust me. Next, think about five things you love about yourself. DO NOT name your physical attributes (ex: I have beautiful brown eyes,

I'm loving my lashes, etc.) Look beneath the surface. If I were standing beside you right now, I would say, "Girlfriend, look at your strength and everything you have overcome. You are bold, courageous, intelligent, funny, and mad cool. Why? Because those are the things we tend to overlook. What do you love about you? Look in the mirror and tell yourself the five things you love about you.

Wait! Don't walk away from the mirror yet. Let's address those insecurities. (You know we had to go there.) For this part of the exercise, think about five things you dislike about yourself. You can even refer to the list you made in Facet One. Here's the trick. Instead of saying that you don't like these things, say, "I love *insert your insecurity here*" This helps us to appreciate everything about ourselves. For me, I don't like my feet. I've had to learn to love them because they aren't going anywhere. What do I do now to appreciate them more? I make sure they are polished and pedicured. Regardless of what they look like, they are mine, and they are serving their purpose.

Don't get me wrong. There are somethings we can do to change certain things about ourselves. For instance, if we don't like our weight, we can develop a healthier lifestyle. If we don't like how shy we are, we can do a little personal development and challenge ourselves to learn how to make friends. Nevertheless, in the meantime, we must love ourselves right where we are, the way we are.

Lord,

I'm grateful for every part of me -- the parts I love, and the parts I don't like as much. Teach me how to affirm myself daily. Teach me to love myself the way you created me. As I learn to affirm myself daily, show me how to speak positive affirmations over those who are connected to me. Thank you for showing me how to fall in love with my dopeness. God, I ask that you heal me from any past insecurities. Teach me how to love my flaws and all. I love you, and thank you. It's in Jesus Christ's name I pray. Amen!

How can you appreciate the things you don't like about you?

How can you affirm the areas you love about yourself?

FACET
Three

"Positivity is Key."

Before I found myself and began to seek God about my life, I ALWAYS spoke negatively about every situation. I would say stuff like, "I'm probably going to be broke. I will never have children. He probably will cheat on me." You could come around me and be having a marvelous day, but, honey, my middle name was misery. I was unhappy with my life, who I had become, and where my life was heading. In addition to hating being single and a plethora of other things, I lost my parents too early for my liking. So, I walked around pissed off about everything. I was quick to snap on people, no matter how nice and sweet they were to me. I never smiled and wasn't approachable. It was awkward to meet people who were always happy. I would ask myself, "Why are they always so happy? What is there to always smile about?"

When I was younger, I had a dream about my funeral. I saw myself in the casket, but no one else was there. I had been such a bad person, that no one wanted to be around me! After seeing that for a couple of years, I knew God was trying to get my attention.

I had to reprogram my thought process. I had to begin to speak differently about my life, even if it wasn't going smoothly. I had to learn to seek God and tell him my frustrations. I had to seek God's word about what I was doing and saying. Proverbs 18:21(MSG) says, "Words kill, words give life; they're either poison or fruit — you choose." God is a G! You hear me? He had to deal with me about changing my verbiage and protecting my eye and ear gates (being mindful of the things I listened to and watched.) Since doing so, I have been able to produce more good fruit in my life. I even have people that rock with me the long way. I speak positive thoughts daily, and I'm cautious about the things I say. Trust me, sis. Making these adjustments will change your entire life. Of course, there are days I get discouraged. On those days, I chose to remind myself of how God sees me, and that he will allow everything to work together for my good.

Father,

Thank you for positive thoughts. Thank you for reprogramming my mindset. Thank you for the shifting of my thoughts. I come against every demonic attack that tries to keep my thoughts negative. Protect my eye and ear gates. Fill me with positive thoughts. Teach me how to love individuals who try to keep me down from a distance. Rebuke every trick of the enemy, and teach me how to win the battle in my mind! Thank you in advance for the people who are coming to pour positivity into my life. Thank you for your mercy and your grace. In your name we pray! Amen!

FACET
Four

"Sis. Stop Comparing."

Comparison is the worst form of bondage for women. It's dangerous and down-right evil. Comparison will have you wanting to cry, pull your hair out, run to a corner, suck your thumb, and tell God, "I give up!" Comparison is the act or instance of comparing or measuring the similarities or differences between two or more people, items, etc. Need me to make it a little clearer? As women, we often look at other women and say crazy things like, "Why doesn't my life look like hers? I wish I had her shape. I'm not as pretty as she is. When will I meet a man like her husband? How is she so popular, and I'm not?" We've all been guilty of this at least once or twice in our lives. When you find yourself saying stuff like this, you have to stop and think. Do you know the amount of hell she had to go through to get to the level she is on? Do you know the sacrifices she had to make? Do you know how many times she cried about things not going according to her plan? Do you know how many times she second-guessed herself when others told her how awesome she is? Do you know how many times she thought she couldn't do it? The point is, we have no idea about the back story of the women we compare ourselves to. The best thing for us to do is celebrate our sisters and wait as God allows us to process through our level up as well.

I bet you are thinking, "Yea. It's easy for you to say

that. You've released a whole book!" Don't let the optics fool you. I talked myself out of writing this book more times than I care to mention. I often felt insecure, and like no one wanted to read my advice. I pushed through because I wanted to obey God and help women all around the world. When you saw my big smile on the back of the book cover, you couldn't tell that I'd gone through hell and high waters to produce the words on these pages. You see, a lot of women live by the code my grandmother gave me, "Child, no matter what you are going through, don't ever allow yourself to look like it." That's the secret behind many of the polished women we compare ourselves to on social media, news, tv, and even the women we see on a daily. Yes, you may see a woman strutting her stuff with her head held high, but you have no idea what it took for her to get out of the bed this morning. Again, don't compare yourself to her. Celebrate her for having the strength to pull it together and confidently win the day!

    Don't get me wrong. I've fallen victim to comparison too. I would say things like, "My life is not going right because it doesn't look like hers." I had to learn that any day above ground is always a good day. Every time we wake up with breath in our body, we have another chance to address our faults, improve our lives, and take another step towards being the women God called us to be. Jeremiah 29:11(NIV) says, "For I know the plans

I have for you," declares the Lord, "plans to prosper you and not to harm you, plans to give you hope and a future." This scripture alone lets us know that God has great plans for our lives. He plans to prosper each of us. So we do not need to compare our lives to others! God has an individual plan for us. This scripture helped me to overcome my comparison habits. I made it personal, put my name in there, and said out loud, "For GOD knows the plans HE has for ADRIENNE. He plans to prosper ADRIENNE and not to harm ADRIENNE. HE plans to give ADRIENNE hope and a future. I encourage you to place your name in the scripture and read it aloud! As a matter of fact, do this with every scripture that inspires you and reminds you of God's promises for your life.

The real reason many women fall into comparison is because things aren't happening the way we want, and as fast as we want them to happen. Can I be honest with you, sis? This is a control issue, and many women have this problem. We are daughters of The Most High God. He wants us to relinquish our control, submit to His plan, and watch as He does a great work in our lives. When we are able to do this, we can stop comparing our lives to the next person. Actually, we'll be too busy on our journey with God that we won't have time to look around and see what everyone else is doing. I know you are ready for your legal bae, the kids, the career, and the house with the privacy fence. God knows you desire those things. In His timing, He will allow your desires to manifest in your life. Just trust His plan, obey His instructions, and allow God to be God. Believe me, He knows what's best!

Finally, sis, I want to leave you with this scripture. Philippians 1:6 (ESV) says, "And I am sure of this, that he who began a good work in you will bring it to completion at the day of Jesus Christ." God is perfecting you and preparing you for everything you desire. It's all going to work out! Drive in your lane because the next person's lane is already occupied! Be done with comparison. You are AMAZING, and God's plan for your life is BEAUTIFUL!

Lord,

Help me as I work hard to stop comparing my life to others. Silence the insecurities that tell me that I am not worthy. Give me the strength to celebrate what you are doing in the lives of others instead of comparing myself to their success. Affirm me, Father. Open my eyes to see how you are working in my life. Keep me focused on the task you've specifically called me to do. Teach me to enjoy the process and to learn what you want to reveal to me in this season. Help me stay focused on what you have called me to do within the Earth. Thank you, Lord, and it's in your name I pray! Amen!

What are some things you feel you are lacking?

What ways have you compared yourself to others?

FACET
Five

"Support Your Sister!"

As women, we can be so competitive sometimes! In addition to comparing ourselves to other women, we are also guilty of talking bad about the next woman. We talk about how she hustles or not, we belittle her because she is "doing too much," or even throw shade her way. Why though? Most of the time, it's because we are jealous, and we don't know how to appreciate other women without feeling bad about our own lives. Ouch. I know that may be a hard pill to swallow, but it's the truth. Don't turn the page! We've got to talk about this, sis. With all that's going on in the world, the last thing we need to do is hate on other women.

I'm going to be completely honest here. There are women I have been jealous of. I compared my looks to theirs, their hustle to mine, and their confidence to my low self-esteem. I would even turn my nose up at other women who were out here grinding. Why? Because I couldn't understand their drive and I didn't have the same drive. I would not support them out of jealousy. One day I had to realize that instead of being jealous, I should admire my sisters. Instead of comparing, I needed to acknowledge the qualities about her I liked, and fix my life. Not to become a replica of other women, but to grow in my own lane. Instead of hating, I needed to learn from my sister and apply those lessons to my

Facet Five: Support Your Sister!

life and personality.

Now I've been real about my jealousy issues. Let's talk about you. Have you ever had a conversation with yourself and said, "If only I had her personality, her style, her car, or even her hair, then I would do this or that?" It is okay to admire certain things about other women, but those things shouldn't keep us from loving and supporting each other and ourselves. We have to learn how to look at other women and admire that they may be relatable, cool, funny, and dope as hell! We should be able to acknowledge our sisters' hustle and beauty without feeling bad about our own. We should be able to support our sisters even when things aren't going so well in our own lives.

So how do we get to this place? I'm glad you asked. It begins with honesty. Once we are honest with ourselves, some things become easier. Instead of hating and being jealous, get to the root of the issue! Why do you have such a problem with other women? What do you wish you could do better in your own life? Honesty will allow you to face the truth, and instead of being her enemy, put your pride to the side and become a student. Then, take what you learn and help another sister along your journey. Do you see how that works? When we learn to admire and support each other, we not only benefit ourselves but other sisters we come in contact with.

Before we close out, let's talk a little bit more about how to support our sisters. If I could insert a scream here, I would! It breaks my heart to see how we refuse to support our sisters in Christ, but have the audacity to be upset when other women don't support us. Supporting one another isn't just something we do; it's God's desire for His children to love and support each other. Don't believe me? Let's look at Galatians 5:14-15 (TPT):

"For love completes the laws of God. All of the law can be summarized in one grand statement: Demonstrate love to your neighbor, even as you care for and love yourself. But if you continue to criticize and come against each other over minor issues, you're acting like wild beasts trying to destroy one another."

Before you give me the long list of why you don't support certain women, let me let you know that I've heard it all before! We say things like, "I won't support her because her prices are too high, she takes too long, or I just don't think she has what it takes." In this season, I'm learning that when we don't support each other, we aren't doing Kingdom business. We are partaking into the world's shenanigans. God wants us to help bring people to him, and most connections are made through business partnerships and fellowship. We are out here playing. Some of my best connections have come from supporting the next woman. Learn to put your personal differences aside and support her, sis. You never know how it will work in your favor!

For my sisters who have been on the other end and have had to deal with jealous or mean women, keep doing you, boo! The truth is, some women are intimidated by the next woman because confident women carry qualities that intimidated women don't have. Don't dim your light for those who don't know how awesome they are yet! Keep being the light that others see so they can make changes in their lives. Shine in love, and don't allow it to make you bitter or mean towards other women. We are all in a process, so pray for your sisters! One day, we will all understand how to be inspired by each other's strength.

Dear Father,

I come against any spirit of comparison and hate within me. Teach me how to love and support other women. Father, I ask that when I begin to speak of not wanting to support my sisters, remind me to do a self-evaluation to see why I may feel this way. Soften my heart to volunteer and serve with other businesses, ministries, and organizations with my sisters in Christ. Lord, because you have called for us to be servants, I ask that you teach me how to support and serve willingly. Thank you for what you're doing and how you're changing my life. I love you, and thank you! Amen!

What can you do to support other women?

How would you like other women to support you?

FACET
Six

"Let That Grudge Go, Girl!"

Has someone ever hurt you or done you wrong, and you decided to be done with them? Honey, this was my story. I was the queen of holding grudges and being done with people! I could ignore someone so well that they would start to question if they really existed. I'm not proud of it, but this was how I dealt with hurt. You see, I'm the type of person who gives people so many chances to get it right before I cut them off. (Remember, I have a huge heart.) After a person refuses to change, I release them. While there's nothing wrong with that, my problem was learning to forgive and release. All I did was release!

As I further examined my behavior, I also realized that my tolerance level was different for different people. When it came to the men I was having sex with, I let them slide, even though they didn't change. On the other hand, other people who were close to me would get the business if they offended me. Don't look like that! You're probably guilty of this too, sis. Just think about it. We can get mad with bae and be over it with one phone call and some flowers. But if we have a fall out with our girlfriends, we ignore each other for months. I know so many women who are still with the same no good man but aren't talking to their loved ones because of something petty.

As I was writing this chapter, God gave me even

Facet Six: Let that Grudge Go, Girl!

more revelation about myself and why a lot of women are like this. Those that I kept giving chances were mostly strangers or my "chill buddies." I felt like they didn't know any better, so I was more tolerant. I felt like because they didn't know me, I had to teach them how to treat me. I felt like the people who knew me and were closer, should have known not to piss me off. This was my mentality. I felt like because we were cool, they should have known me and my triggers. Can you relate? As much as this may make sense to us, the truth is, it's unrealistic. No matter how long people have known you, it's possible that they can hurt you or do something to offend you. It's impossible to go through life without being offended. So, do you know what we've got to do? We have to learn how to forgive and release those grudges.

    I get it. Sometimes, when people do something we don't like, we feel obligated to treat them any kind of way and hold grudges against them. However, this isn't how God would like us to operate with each other. And, since we're being honest, holding grudges is sometimes our way of manipulating people to do what we want them to do.

    Since I've grown and matured, I had to realize how important it is to let go of grudges. Did you know that holding grudges can block your blessings? The truth is, some of the grudges we are holding against others are petty and tedious. I don't know about you, but I don't want the things I've been praying for to be held up because of a silly grudge. Also, we have to take a look in the mirror. We are not perfect, and there are some people that we have offended as well. Wouldn't you want those people to forgive you for your mistakes? When I realized this, I started letting go of grudges and apologizing left and right. As a matter of fact, if you are reading this book and I've ever done you wrong, I apologize for any hurt that I have caused you. Those were not my intentions. Will you forgive me?

When we allow God to mature us, we are able to look at situations and learn to communicate any frustrations or issues we may have, instead of holding a grudge. We learn to be gracious towards each other. Before you go to the next facet, take a look at Ephesians 4:31-32 (NIV). It says, "Get rid of all bitterness, rage, and anger, brawling and slander, along with every form of malice. Be kind to one another tenderhearted, forgiving one another, as God in Christ forgave you."

So there it is, sis! We forgive because we have been forgiven. Let's pray.

Lord,

Forgive me for the grudges I have held against others. Teach me how to forgive others freely and quickly. Remove any negative feelings I may have towards people. Your word says in Matthew 6:12 (NIV), "And forgive us our debts, as we also have forgiven our debtors." God, the same way you forgave those that crucified you, I ask that you give me the tools I need to forgive those that come against me. God, I know that holding grudges leaves me bitter, mean, and unwelcoming. Remove those traits from me. I thank you in advance for the changes that are about to take place in my heart. Thank you, Father, for your grace and your love. In the mighty name of Jesus! Amen!

Is there anyone you're holding a grudge against? What did they do? Why haven't you forgiven them?

FACET
Seven

"Manage Your Emotions Well."

When God gave me the title of this chapter, I instantly wanted to get in my feelings! I mean, we are women, and we have emotions, right? Most people say we are emotional creatures, and, ladies, I've got to agree. We cry at the drop of a hat. We can be moody. We are sweet and sour. We can be sensitive. I know I can testify to this. I am passionate about a lot of things, I can be emotional, my heart is huge, I tend to let a lot of things bother me, and I can be impatient. While I can admit these things about myself, I'm learning how to refrain from inflicting those emotions onto others.

In addition to those of us who are a bit much when expressing our emotions, there are those who don't show any emotions at all. If that's you, then understand, you too have to learn how to manage your emotions. Not showing emotions doesn't mean you are managing your emotions well. The thing is, we are supposed to have and show emotions. Let me ask you something. Why are you afraid of showing your emotions? Are you afraid to be vulnerable with other women or people in general? Do you have trust issues? I've been there as well. I once had a very hard exterior. My facial expressions were never welcoming, and I wasn't very friendly. Honestly, this was a defense mechanism for me. It was my way of keeping people from getting too close to me. I didn't want anyone to sense what I was really dealing with, you know, my real emotions.

After dealing with this for so long, I knew it was time to change these habits. I said to myself, "Girl, stop playing and mature in this area." As I began to deal with my hard exterior, I uncovered the roots of my "tough girl" issues. A few years ago, I dated a guy who told me I was too emotional for him, and he couldn't be with me. Even though I tried to change, it wasn't good enough for him. Even though he left, I kept that tough girl exterior. This, in addition to many other events in my life, caused me to harden my heart and keep my emotions boxed in.

Sometimes, we go through things, and when the situation ends, we are left with the effects of it. Think about it. When did you start masking your emotions? What made you feel like having emotions was a negative thing? Who made you feel weak for expressing your emotions? As you take time to think about this, you will begin to heal from those situations and take back your right to your emotions.

Going on the journey of learning how to properly manage my emotions has been the most beautiful journey. I watched in awe as my display of emotions matured. Before I would only cry if I was sad, mad, frustrated, or feeling some type of way because of a movie. I was very insecure, so if I felt like someone was talking about me, I would get into my feelings.

If someone said something with a certain tone or authority, it would hurt my feelings. If someone looked at me the wrong way, then I would probably cry or shut down. Now I find myself crying because of how good God is and the connections he has brought into my life. This doesn't mean that I only felt positive things. I still dealt with negative emotions, I just knew how to manage them. When I felt angry, I remembered that Proverbs 15:1(NIV) says, "A gentle answer turns away wrath, but a harsh word stirs up anger." When I felt nervous or anxious, I remembered that Philippians 4:6 tells me to be anxious for nothing. When I felt sad, I remembered Psalm 30:5 that tells us that weeping may endure for a night, but joy comes in the morning. Remember how I told you I hated confrontation? Now, I'm not afraid it face it head on, because I know how to turn it into a positive.

    Ladies, our emotions help us to be compassionate, nurturing, and caring to name a few. We should never be embarrassed by our emotions. They make us unique. We do, however, need to ensure that we have a handle on our emotions. Our emotions should never be used to manipulate, hurt, or cause harm to others. We are supposed to have emotions, however, our emotions should not have us! Our emotions should never cause us to make temporary decisions that will have a negative outcome for the rest of our lives.

Facet Seven: Manage Your Emotions Well

Dear Lord,

Thank you for allowing me to be in control of my emotions. If there are some past traumas I haven't healed from, bring them back into my remembrance so I can address them. God, I want to be in control of my emotions and not succumb to my emotions. Strengthen me in the weakened areas. Your word says in Philippians 4:7 (KJV), "And the peace of God, which passeth all understanding, shall keep your hearts and your minds in Christ Jesus." I will not allow my emotions to run wild, but I will seek you first. Help me to do as your word says in Colossians 3:2 (NIV), "Set your mind on the things above, not on earthly things." Lord, thank you in advance for how you will help me manage my emotions. Lord, I bless you and thank you. Amen!

Are you overly emotional? What are your triggers?

Do you struggle with suppressing your emotions? When did this begin?

FACET
Eight

"A Mother's Love"

This topic is very touchy for me. Unfortunately, I didn't get to experience a mother's love like some girls because I was raised by my father. Don't get me wrong. There was nothing wrong with being raised by my daddy. I was a true daddy's girl. However, every girl needs a woman present in her life, especially in our early developmental years. We need a woman to teach us about puberty, menstrual cycles, boobs, our "miss peach," and so much more. As a grown woman, I'm still learning things I should have learned as a teenager. Even though I'm getting some lady lessons late, God knew exactly what I needed, when I needed it. I had a lot of great experiences with my father and saw more than some children will ever see in their lifetime. Nevertheless, as a young girl, I needed my mother.

I thank God for keeping me and allowing me to become the woman I am today. I am so very grateful, as there were times when I wondered if I would ever learn how to be nice and get over the hurt of my mother not being present in my life. Honestly, I didn't start dealing with the things that hurt me until I turned 35 years old. I never allowed anyone to come into my life to help me address my mother issues.

When I think back on it, it was probably good that my parents split. As a little girl, I remember sitting in a corner, wishing my parents would stop fighting.

Facet Eight: A Mother's Love

Sometimes, it felt like that was all they did -- in addition to drinking. Party. Fight. Drink. Sometimes, I would hide in the closet to get away from all the commotion and constant fighting. To make matters worse, police officers were always at our home in Atlanta to break up their fights. I even had a picture of an officer holding me during one of their "house calls" to our residence.

Finally, after the constant fighting and arguments, my parents decided they were too toxic for each other. We all went from Atlanta, Georgia to Mobile, Alabama, where both of my parents were from. Later on, my dad and I moved to Huntsville, Alabama. When we moved, I remember struggling with being without my mother. It hurt me to see women and their daughters together. It hurt knowing that God allowed my mother to choose alcohol over me. My maternal grandmother told my dad that I would live a better life with him, but I didn't understand why my mother didn't fight for me.

After some time, I grew to dread visiting my mother in Atlanta. I didn't feel safe, and I believe I had some hate and resentment in my heart towards her. One day, I made the decision to stop talking to her. We didn't communicate or see each other for years. When I turned 17 or 18 years old, we began communicating again. One year, I went to visit her, and things got bad. She allowed her alcohol to start talking for her and accused me of sleeping with my stepfather. One thing led to another, and she was charging at me. I jumped in, and it became a fistfight. I mean, we thumped! That hurt me so bad. Never in a million years did I think my mother and I would physically fight. We eventually got over our fight and started to repair our relationship. Six years after that fight, God decided he was ready to call her home! I didn't understand. We were just starting to develop a real relationship. This broke my heart.

Even though I didn't want to be like my parents, I drifted down the same road. I would party, drink, and smoke weed daily. One day, I decided that I was done with that lifestyle. I realized that if I didn't want to be like my parents, I needed to make different decisions. For many years, I harbored hurt, regret, rejection, and abandonment issues in my heart. As I began my healing process, I realized that I had been suppressing my emotions towards my mother. I didn't realize how much I was hurting until God spoke to me through someone at church one Wednesday. I had to release that hurt I'd been lying to myself about. I had to accept that my mother loved me the best way she knew how.

That pain I was holding on to made me afraid of having children. I feared that they would lose me like I lost my mother. God told me that even though I lost my mother, that doesn't mean I won't be an awesome mother to my children. Now, my declaration is that I will live, and God has already designed me with the "loving mother" trait! In addition to forgiving my mother, I had to forgive myself for holding grudges against her in my heart.

Ephesians 4:32 (ESV) says, "Be kind to one another, tenderhearted, forgiving one another, as God in Christ forgave you." Regardless of what we go through with our mothers, we must remember that she is not perfect, and she is only human. She will make mistakes. Just like I had to remember that I wasn't perfect, and I made mistakes as a daughter.

Losing my mother was one of the hardest things I have faced to date. If you still have your mother around, do your best to forgive her and build a healthy relationship. Already have a strong relationship? That's beautiful! Let your mother know that you appreciate her today!

As for my ladies who, like me, lost your mother, or didn't have the best relationship with your mother, I challenge you to allow God to heal your heart. Even though it may have been tough, thank God for the time you had with your mother. Try to find the beauty in the relationship that you had. Rest assured that if your desire is to be a mother, God will allow it to manifest in His timing. You will be an amazing mother. Far from perfect, but your children will love and cherish you. Can I pray for all of us?

Lord,

I thank you for the mothers reading this book. Father, I pray for any reconciliations that need to take place amongst mothers and daughters. I pray that you restore relationships that have become estranged. I pray for this generation of women and the mother's love that each woman possesses. I pray that each woman finds strength in her weaknesses. I pray that she laughs at the thought of the future. I pray she shows Satan that he can't stop her because she has been made in the image of God. I pray you give each woman the strength to be present in their child/ren lives. I pray that you give her power each day to stay planted in their lives. I pray that you teach them how to continue to push through even on the most challenging days. We love and thank you in advance for what you're doing. Amen!

Do you need to repair your relationship with your mom?

What do you feel like you want to say to your mother about building a better relationship with her?

FACET Nine

"BUT GOD!"

God is the ultimate reason why I'm still here. Have you ever heard someone say, "I wasn't supposed to be here..."BUT GOD!" Or, "The devil tried to take me out..."BUT GOD!" From birth until now, my life has been one big, "BUT GOD!" testimony! During my delivery, my head was too big for my mama's pelvic region. Her doctor, who was in a rush to get to another hospital in Atlanta, used forceps to get me out. Of course, this caused head trauma. A mistake like this should have caused me to have unclear speech, slow mental processes, and limited use of my limbs.....you guessed it..."BUT GOD!" All I have today is a scar on the right side of my face. In a season of my life where I wasn't as aware of how much of a walking miracle I was, God allowed me to hear about a young man who had experienced the same thing as me during birth. Unfortunately, his abilities were limited and had to depend on others for his essential needs. Hearing about this story made me realize how blessed I am to be here today. I realized that my turn-out wasn't a mere coincidence. It was nothing but the goodness of God.

Have you ever heard about the woman with the issue of blood? She bled for 12 years, and when Jesus was walking by, she touched the hem of his robe. Instantly she stopped bleeding. (Luke 8:43-48). The amazing thing about this story is that this woman shouldn't have been anywhere near people, especially not Jesus. You see, in those days and times, women were ordered out of the public when they dealt with issues like this woman. She was considered unclean…"BUT GOD!" Her desperation to be healed and God's timing allowed her to be in the right place at the right time. In a matter of moments, her story changed from trial to triumph!

I don't know every detail of your life, however, I know you have a "BUT GOD!" story somewhere in your timeline. This journey we call life is not comfortable. You will have times when you feel helpless. You will doubt everything. You will go through seasons where you can't see when or if the light will come. It is in those seasons you need to remember your "BUT GOD!" story. You have to remind yourself that if God pulled your through before, surely, he doesn't mind doing it again. Why would He bring you this far, just to bring you this far?

If you are still in a place where you are struggling with your relationship with God, and you have a hard time letting Him in, can I convince you today to give him a try? Before I allowed God into my situation, I was bitter, mean, insecure, impatient, and a plethora of other things. I'm not perfect today, but I am in a place where I am allowing God's grace, love, kindness, and mercy to perfect me. I can say this has been the best decision I have ever made. All He wants us to do is trust Him with all of us. Yes, sis, God wants all of you and not part of you. That means the things we value: Our families, job, finances, business, and just our whole being. He wants the broken, not so cute parts, too. Only in His hands can all things, everything you've been through, work together for your good. Will you give yourself to him? Don't you want to add to your "BUT GOD!" testimonies? Let me pray for you!

Dear God,

I pray for every woman who has lost herself. I pray for the woman who doesn't feel worthy of your love, and I also pray for those who second guess who they are. Father, I pray that each woman finds the love that only you can give. Help her to embrace every struggle and/or tragedy that has happened in their life. Help her to see how she has overcome those situations. May she realize that it's only by your strength that she is still here! May she find herself giving you a "BUT GOD" praise. Help her to see herself as you see her. I pray that she will begin evaluating the many circumstances in her life that she has escaped. Help her to see how you have kept her over the years. Lord, we thank you for your blessings, and it's in your name we pray! Amen!

Facet Nine: BUT GOD!

What are your "But God" moments?

FACET
Ten

"Just Be Free!
You know you want to be."

One of the hardest things I struggled with was trying to please EVERYONE! Growing up, I was considered mean because "I didn't take no junk from nobody." Okay, let me be honest for a moment. I guess I was mean to a certain extent. I have always been and will always be a woman who does not tolerate nonsense. I have a zero-tolerance for bull crap! When I sense that people are full of it, I don't deal with those people. People have misunderstood me for years, but those who get me, love me. I've always been the type of person who says how I feel with no filter. Well, somewhere along my journey, people's opinions began to hurt me. The things people said, the way they looked at me, what they told others about me behind my back started to dictate how I saw myself. Over time, I became a version of what everyone thought I should be. I altered who I was as a person so that people would change their narrative about me.

Ladies, we aren't perfect. And, we aren't everyone's flavor. With that being said, people will, at some point, tell you a thing or two about yourself that you may not like. Step One, don't fool yourself into thinking that you don't care what people say about you. I thought the same thing until I found myself crying in my pillow, wondering why certain people didn't like me. Be honest and real with yourself and deal with your emotions. Step

Two. Before you make one single adjustment, go to God directly. Ask him to reveal the truth in what was said to you. Ask God if there is something you need to change, not so you can become what they desire. Rather, so that you can become the woman God had in mind when he created you. Ask God to give you the fruits of the spirit. Galatians 5:22 (KJV) says, "but the fruit of the Spirit is love, joy, peace, long-suffering, gentleness, goodness, faith, meekness, temperance; against such there is no law."

See, at that time, I didn't understand the importance of going to the Bible to get a better understanding of who I was and whose I was. I just changed and prayed that my changes would make people like me. Then, I felt like I became soft because I was trying to appease people. I was allowing people to run over me, and I wouldn't say anything. This became a problem because I never felt like myself. I was starting to become what and who people wanted me to be.

Let's fast forward to 2019. I was talking to one of my homies from Memphis. We were talking about some everyday stuff, how to survive in this world of entrepreneurship, and some other things. He told me something that I will carry with me for life. He said, "You know, once you really get delivered from the opinions of others, that will be the day you have a different type of freedom." I began thinking about what he said, and I was like, "Dang. He is so right." That statement shook me, and I realized that I'd been living my life all wrong. "Why am I worried about what people have to say about me? The only person I need to worry about approving me is God!" I thought to myself. Ever since that day, I have been working on this diligently. I'm free from the opinions of others! I'm free of people trying to tell me who I am, who they think I should be, how I should do things, and what they feel is best for me! I'm free from people trying to tell me how to act, I'm free from their views of me, and I'm free of people-pleasing! For me to get here, I had to allow God into those places that I allowed other people's opinions to settle. I had to ask him to remove the residue of what I allowed to harbor there and replace those areas with Him!

You can experience this freedom too! Start with being open and honest with God about the things you want to change and where you currently are in life. God already knows, so I would suggest that you not lie. Freedom takes some work and a lot of sacrificing, but it's worth it.

Remember, Queens, people will judge you based on their insecurities. Don't live your life based on man. Live it based on The Man: Jesus Christ! As John 8:36 (ESV) says, "If the Son sets you FREE, you will be FREE indeed!" Let's pray!

Dear Heavenly Father,

Thank you for my newfound freedom. Thank you for not allowing me to be conformed to this world and renewing my mind. Help me to walk freely, talk freely, laugh freely, love freely, and speak freely. Lord, I will not be confined to my inner person. I will not go into isolation because I fear the opinions of others. I will not think less of myself because I know I am the Daughter of the King. I will be free to laugh and dance. Father, I ask that you send me people who are also free in you. Lord, I thank you and bless your name. Amen!

Where are some areas in your life that you desire to be free?

What's holding you back?

FACET
Eleven

"Are you well-fed or well-nourished?"

Crown Her Diamond

Have you ever gone out with your girls for a girl's night out, and you couldn't decide what to eat? You looked over the menu several times but still couldn't decide. You find something that looks good, but then you decide you really don't want anything too heavy, so you pick out a couple of appetizers to hold you over until later. Then later comes, and you realize how hungry you are because you decided to eat light, and then you feel like you are starving. This is because the things you consumed had no real substance. Yes, girl. Those appetizers were basically wasted calories. I don't know about you, but if I'm going to eat anything, it had better fill me and satisfy me!

Now, let's think about this in regards to what we consume on the daily! I'm not talking about food anymore. I'm talking about the TV shows we watch, the movies we pay to see at the theaters, the music we jam to, and the conversations of the people we surround ourselves with. After indulging in too much junk, we find ourselves too depleted to do the things that will take us places in life! What's even worse, the things we are consuming don't fill us or give us the energy, strength, or discipline we need to live lives that are pleasing to God.

Don't get me wrong. I love a good movie and a good show. Martin, to be exact. Martin is one of my all-

Facet Eleven: Well-Fed or Well-Nourished?

time favorite shows. I love the Cosby Show, CSI, the ID channel, Lifetime, and The Fresh Prince, to name a few. I've never been a big rap fan, but I would listen to Tupac, Twista, or Mystikal back in my younger days. See, I am a TRUE R&B fan. My mom and dad listened to vinyl's when I was growing up, so I was exposed to Anita Baker, the Temptations, Marvin Gaye, Gladys Knight, and many other greats at a young age. I know good music! However, there are some songs I just can't listen to — especially during my single season. What happens is the music gets good, my mind starts to wander, and before I know it, lust begins to set in. Now I'm going to be completely honest with you. Depending on where I was in my headspace, and if alcohol was involved, I would go somewhere and start masturbating and watching porn. That was something I felt like I needed because of the things I was letting in my ear and eye gates. God made me give up sex, so I tried to compromise my need. I would justify why I needed to supplement the urge, so it would give me a reason to masturbate. When I wrote this book, I had been abstinent for four years. That was not an easy journey. For a while, I couldn't listen to R&B because of how it tempted me. The stronger I became, and the more I allowed God to perfect me, R&B music lost its power over me. Now, I still listen to R&B music but with control. I know what my triggers are, and I no longer masturbate or watch porn.

Are the things you are consuming nourishing your spirit man? Do they make you a better person? Do they motivate you to dream big? Do they keep you in alignment with God's instruction for your life? Much of the things we struggle with are because of what we choose to consume. Sure, you can say that music, social media, and television aren't affecting you, but take a look at yourself. Do you call your friends the B-word? When you look at yourself in the mirror, do you compare yourself to women you see on Instagram or Facebook? Do you crave relationships like the ones you hear about in love songs? I challenge you to take a look at your behavior and actions and see if it aligns with anything you've been consuming.

I'm not trying to force the Bible down your throat, but you will notice a major change in your life when you choose to consume more of God's word. You won't have to force yourself to change. As the Word of God becomes a part of your daily diet, you will transform. It won't be an easy process. Your taste buds will change. Your desires will change. And most importantly, your circles will change. I remember going through this, and it wasn't the most comfortable season of my life. Nevertheless, I can look back and say that I'm glad I changed my diet! I have great friendships and positive relationships. I am able to motivate myself when I'm feeling down. I love the skin I'm in. All of this came about when I decided to change what I was consuming.

The woman God desires you to be is right on the other side of your decision to change your diet! Just as with any nutrition plan, start gradually and work your way up! Choose some worship music instead of your favorite rap song at the gym. Instead of watching a reality show, search YouTube for an inspirational message. When you want to turn up with the homies, chose to settle in for a quiet evening with God. Watch as your life begins to transform! Now, this doesn't mean that you can't have fun. Because, believe me, I love the Lord, but I still like to have a good twerk session with my girls every now and then, mmkay! It's all in moderation. Just like with your diet, sweets and salty food aren't bad, but too much isn't good for you. Load up on the good stuff, and limit your intake of everything else!

God,

Thank you for allowing me to be in control of the things I take in. I ask that you begin to show me how certain things affect me, whether good or bad. Do a new thing within me and show me how you desire to use me. God, help me to maintain the things that I consume. Reveal to me how the things I consume may impact the generations that come behind me. Help me to be open to change. I want to be properly fed by the things I take in. Help me recognize my triggers, and give me the strength to flee from temptation. Father, I desire to still have fun, but show me how to make Your Word and positivity the main part of my diet! Reveal to me anything that may hinder my walk with you. I love you, and thank you. It's in your name I pray. Amen!

FACET
Twelve

"Find Your Fire, Boo!"

Did you know you were created for a divine purpose? Do you know you are the answer to a problem? Did you know you were designed uniquely for a reason? Have you ever heard the scripture, "Before I formed you in the womb, I knew you, before you were born, I set you apart; I appointed you as a prophet to the nations?" Jeremiah 1:5(NIV). There is a particular anointing that has been placed on each of our lives. It's up to us if we are going to walk in the full authority of who we were created to be. There is a fire at the pit of your soul, and it needs to come out.

For many years, I resented the calling on my life. I had a specific path already planned for my life, but of course, that wasn't God's plan. I wanted to live my life as I wanted to and walk around with this whole victim mentality. Yup, that's right! I wanted to walk around and say, "Woe, is me!"

During a trip to Chicago, I was walking through a train station trying to get to my hotel, when I saw a woman in a wheelchair asking for money. At that moment, God began to speak to me about what happens when we don't apply ourselves. As I was telling my friend the revelation God revealed to me, it weighed even heavier on me. I realized that God was trying to get me to see that the victim mentality would not serve me or the purpose He had for my life. It was time for me to drop the "woe is me" verbiage and learn to speak the language of where God was taking me.

Sometimes, we choose to stay in our victim roles for far too long. We will blame outside sources for why our lives are the way they are. When the truth of the matter is, sometimes, we are to blame. We have to choose to apply ourselves and push past the demanding situations that have occurred in our lives.

What if I told you that God created everything that you've gone through for his divine glory? You may ask, "What does that mean, Adrienne?" Jeremiah 29:11(NLT) says, "for I know the plan I have for you, says the Lord. They are plans for good and not for disaster, to give you a future and a hope." God knew the plans he had for you since the foundation of the world. That's right. Before you were even a thought in your mother's mind, God had a plan for you. Every part of your life was planned and scheduled. Nothing you've been through has taken God by surprise. He is using everything you have gone through to perfect you and position you for the destiny He created for you.

Let me tell you a story about three people, Shadrach, Meshack, and Abednego. If you don't know who they are, go check out Daniel 3. King Nebuchadnezzar wanted them to serve the same god he did, or he threatened to throw them in a fire pit. Because they served the highest God, they weren't phased about being thrown in the burning fiery furnace. They knew their God would deliver them from the fire. King Nebuchadnezzar was infuriated and demanded that the fire be heated seven times more than it was usually heated. Shadrach, Meshack, and Abednego were then thrown into the burning fiery furnace. Since the king ordered the fire to be increased, it killed the men who took Shadrach, Meshach, and Abednego to the fire. This is where the story gets good! The king looked into the furnace and asked, "Did we not cast three men in the fire? I see four men unbound, walking in the midst of the fire, and they are not hurt; and the appearance of the fourth is like a son of the gods." The men came out of the fire with the hair on their heads not singed, their cloaks were not harmed, and no smell of fire had come upon them. God sent his angel to deliver his servants, who trusted in him, set aside the king's command, and yielded up their bodies rather than serve and worship another god.

Ladies, life can get hot. However, I want to remind you that the fire is not meant to kill you! It will refine you and reveal the glory of God. Everything that you've gone through has a purpose. If you trust God and hold on to His word, you will witness everything work together for your good. If you choose to lay down your victim mentality, God will allow you to live in victory. Be of good courage, hold on to the master's hand, and never let go. The fire around you will only help you understand

Facet Twelve: Find Your Fire, Boo!

your purpose and give you a testimony to share with everyone God places on your path. You, too, will make it out of the fire unharmed and without the residue of what tried to take you out. God only allowed these difficult situations to make you stronger. Keep pushing, lovely. You have what it takes to make it through the fire! Your purpose is counting on it!

Always remember:
1. You have purpose
2. The fire and purpose inside of you will never die unless you allow it to.
3. You are graced for what God created you for.
4. God has great plans for you!

Father,
Thank you for the fire! I am so grateful that what was meant to kill me, made us stronger. God, I believe, just like you sent the angel to walk with Shadrach, Meshach, and Abednego through the fire, you will do the same for me. I won't dread where I am. Instead, I will embrace the journey. I am finding my fire, power, and purpose. Thank you for the grace that covers me as I grow. It's in your name I pray! Amen!

FACET
Thirteen

"Gospel Carrier
or
Gossip Carrier"

Do you find yourself in everyone's business but your own? Are you the girlfriend everyone can count on to keep the "tea" hot? Can I be real with you? If we have the time to sit around and talk about someone else's life, we are probably lacking a life of our own. Anyone who has that much time on their hands to judge what others do can't be fulfilling the purpose they are called to fulfill.

I know, I know. It's not you. It's your friends. Every time you are sitting at home minding your own business, one of your homegirls calls and says, "Girl, did you hear about so and so?" Or "Girl, let me tell you what I heard!" Did I get it right? I know because I blamed my friends for keeping me involved in gossip too. The reality is, if you stay on the phone, that means that you and your crew are unproductive and have very little going for yourselves. The truth hurts, but we've got to deal with this gossip, ladies. The real remedy to gossip is occupying ourselves with what's going on in our own lives.

When I think about gossiping, I'm reminded of a time when I was in high school. Some "friends" and I had gotten together the night of the Super Bowl to watch the game. We were kicking it, laughing, joking, and having a really good time. Well, I had to leave early because I was driving my dad's car and it was a school night. The next day, I got to school and met everyone at the "before class meet up location." I noticed that some of my "friends" were acting funny towards me. At first, I brushed it off until I noticed that everyone in the group was acting funny! Apparently, someone in the group started a rumor and had gossiped about me after I left the Super Bowl party the night before. I'm not going to lie. It hurt my feelings because I couldn't understand what I did to deserve that. I should have learned then to not gossip about others because I didn't like how it made me feel. Unfortunately, we will hang with people that only want to gossip, and we are so easily consumed because we don't have self-control.

Let's take a real look at gossip. How do you think other people feel would feel knowing you have been gossiping about them? Especially those we say we care about? You already know the answer to that question. It will hurt their feelings and destroy their trust in you. Before we choose to gossip, we must think about the people involved. Believe it or not, gossip is the source of many people committing suicide. We never know what people are going through or dealing with. We have to be mindful of people's feelings BEFORE we find out that something terrible has happened to them. As the saying goes these days, the best thing to do is "Mind yo' business and drink yo' water!"

Now the Bible says, Proverbs 16:28 (NLT), "A

troublemaker plants seeds of strife; gossip separates the best of friends." The enemy wants to cause separation amongst those that are supposed to do Kingdom business. Gossip spreads like wildfires, so let's kill it at the spark!

Dear God,

    I'm grateful for the grace you have given me. Thank you for allowing me to come to you with my sins of gossiping. I repent, Father. Thank you for allowing me to try again each day to be better than I was the day before. As I strive to keep away from gossip, guide my thoughts and words. Isaiah 55: 8-9 (NIV) says, "For my thoughts are not your thoughts, neither are your ways my ways," declares the Lord. "As the heavens are higher than the earth, so are my ways higher than your ways and my thoughts than your thoughts." So, Father, I ask that you remove any ways I may have that are not like you. I thank you in advance for the new work that you are about to do in me. I love you, and thank you in advance. Amen!

FACET
Fourteen

"Standards
&
Boundaries"

It's storytime again, ladies! A while back, I was dating this guy, right? Wait, wait, wait. If I'm going to tell this story, I've got to keep it real with y'all! I was having some good sex with this guy, we were playing like we were together, and I was GONE over him. I mean, GONE GONE! Ladies, you know how it is when you get some good sex! I remember telling myself, "Girl, you're going into this with a clear mind, observant, cautious, and with boundaries."

Well, it started that way, but his smile and straight teeth got the best of me. I LOVE a man with straight teeth. He talked that good talk, and he smelled good too. I mean, he said the right things and had "miss peach" purring! I got hoodwinked in a matter of moments. For those that may not know what hookwinked means, it means to be deceived or tricked by someone. I learned quickly that everything that glitters IS NOT GOLD. The game plan I had in my head initially left me at hello, and I never looked back. I was wide open. I got stupid.

I remember telling him how we had to go out on a date first, so we could get to know each other. He agreed until the day we were supposed to go out. I had this feeling he was going to come up with some kind of excuse. He texted me that afternoon and said he was tired from working and wanted me to come over his house instead. This was a red flag for me, but because of this heart of mine, my mind was not working, and I lacked self-control at the time. I went anyway against my better judgment.

Girlfriend, I got to this man's house, and I didn't see a vehicle. I thought to myself, "What in the world is going on here?" I called a friend at the time to let her know where I was and told her that if she didn't hear from me later, she needed to send help!

Ladies, we have gut feelings for a reason. Don't ignore the signs! While I was sitting in front of his house, he texted me to tell me that the front door was unlocked and to come inside because he was in the shower. Red flag #2. "He doesn't know me that well. Why would he just let anyone in his house like that?" This seemed like the perfect set-up, where he could entice me, and get the booty. A man freshly out of the shower and me being horny is one hell of a combination. I knew I should have just started my car up and left. But you know my crazy tail went into the house, right?

So, I sat in this man's house and waited for him to get out of the shower -- on our "first date." He got out of the shower, got dressed, and met me in the living room. We had great conversation that night without sex because I had a meeting to go to that night. If that meeting weren't scheduled, I more than likely would have given him some. I could tell I was attracted to his mind, and he was physically attractive as well.

As the situation-ship continued, I noticed more red flags, less communication, my standards disappeared, and sex made its appearance. Slowly but surely, I found myself slipping into a dark place. I stopped addressing certain things because of his baritone voice. It intimated me. I was almost scared of him because of the aggressiveness he had about himself. See, he was from the streets, so he maneuvered the best way he could to survive. I had been around the streets, but not like he had been. Now he has never put his hands on me, but he was verbally abusive at times. Instead of telling him when he disappointed me, I would take my frustrations out on the people around me that loved me the most.

One weekend, we went to Nashville and were pulled over by the cops. He only had his ID card on him, and we both had been drinking. We got pulled over because his headlights were off. I knew this way before we got pulled over, but I didn't correct him. Needless to say, God spared us because I was able to pass the sobriety test after he failed it.

When we got to the hotel where we were staying, the police officer called me to let me know he had the guy's ID card, and we needed to pick it up from the police station. Do you know this joker let me go out by myself late at night to get his stuff and never said thank you? This is where the game changed for me. Do you know that meme on social media with the little girl holding the small teddy bear, and God has a HUGE one behind his back? At that moment, that's what God was telling me. I was so stuck on sex with him that I had devalued myself. This man even told me to my face that I didn't respect myself or have standards, and you know what? I didn't! I let them go over some good sex.

After I allowed God to finally have my heart and allowed him to heal it, I began to develop better standards. I started to see myself as God saw me. Psalms 139:14 (NKJV) says, "I praise you because I am fearfully and wonderfully made; marvelous are your works, and that my soul knows very well." I had to realize there was more to me than being a baby mama, side chick, or part-time lover. I deserved to be treated with the utmost respect. I also learned that I have to demand those things as well. The man God has for me will see me for the Queen that I am and will only want the best for me! I won't have to beg for his time or attention, but I also plan to treat him like the King he is! We won't be perfect but perfect for each other.

Ladies, I encourage you to look at your current situation and ask yourself, "Does this reflect what God wants for me?" If not, I would encourage you to reevaluate the situation. I want to also encourage the women who are waiting for their bae. If there is a man who is interested in you or potentially interested in you,

HE HAS TO WORK FOR YOU! Don't settle for less than you deserve. Don't give up the cookie! Go out on dates, make him come after you, and respect his efforts. Ladies, we have made it so easy for these men. It's not easy abstaining from someone you're interested in, especially if your heart is anything like mine. Don't be so eager to be in a relationship that you miss what and who God really has for you. Let's pray!

God,
   I pray that each woman reading this sees herself as you see her. Help her to see how wonderful she is and how awesome her personality is. I ask that each morning she gets up and speaks affirmations to herself in the mirror. (I am beautiful, courageous, deserving, intelligent, loving, kind, a wife, a mother, etc.). I pray she never settles for less than what she deserves. Allow her to seek you first to see if the person she is trying to connect with is sent from you. May her relationships portray what you would like people to see in a Godly relationship. God, help her to set boundaries so that she will be able to see who has pure motives and are seeking the best for her. Also, Father, if she is single, I pray that you teach her how to embrace this time alone. May she learn herself and not rush into a relationship just to say she is in one. Father, we thank you and seal this pray with the blood of Jesus. Amen!

Facet Fourteen: Standards and Boundaries

What are some standards you have set in place already or plan on setting for your future?

FACET
Fifteen

"Don't Let Your Cookie Become an Easy Snack!"

How on to your seat, girl! This conversation may get a little graphic. This is me, and this is how I roll. I don't know any other way but to be real with you. I honestly believe that if someone had been this real with me, I would have missed learning lessons the hard way.

When I first started getting serious about my relationship with God, I put everything under lock and key. Clink, Clink! I didn't talk about sex, nor did I acknowledge it. I acted as if I had never gotten busy a day in my life. Prior to this, I was masturbating every day, sometimes multiple times per day. I would watch porn when I needed a good fix, and I had a drawer full of toys. I was satisfied for the moment because God made me stop having sex. If sex was an event, I was in first place. I knew how to do it and do it well. What I didn't realize was there were people who were better at it than me, and I soon found out. This was when I discovered what the meaning of a soul tie really was. I ran up on a man who showed me things I had never seen or experienced before. This situation left me with a soul tie and a broken heart.

I lost my virginity at the age of 17, and I knew sex was going to be my best friend. I loved the way it felt, the pleasure it gave me, and the challenge it made me live up to. If I had a good sex buddy, then it made it even

Facet Fifteen: Your Cookies

more enjoyable for me. Sex became my addiction, and I didn't realize it. I wanted it morning, noon, night, and in between, if I could get it. I was so consumed that I gave it out often, so I could fill a void. I was out here handing my cookie out like those samples you see at the food court in the mall. If the man I wanted to deal with looked good and said the right thing, he could get some. The problem with that was, I ended up with a few curable STD's. After going to the Health Department often and seeing people's files as thick as a dictionary, I knew it was time to change my life. I told myself, "Nope. That is not the life I want to live."

After the last guy I was involved with, God told me it was time to take my cookie back and begin to value myself. He said, "You are more than a snack. You are someone's forever, entrée, and dessert, and it is time you started acting like it!"

I went through a purging phase, and it was hard as hell. I had weak moments where I went back to masturbating to fill that void. God made me throw all of my toys away. I had to stop watching porn. It has been a struggle to get here, but I have been abstinent for almost four years, and it feels amazing. Now don't get me wrong. I can't wait for my husband to get here! Know that it hasn't been easy, but it has been so worth it.

I went through a lot of self-discovery and evaluation

during this process. I had to allow God to remind me that my body is a temple. 1 Corinthians 6:15-20 (NLT) reminds me, "Don't you realize that your bodies are actually parts of Christ? Should a man take his body, which is part of Christ, and join it to a prostitute? Never! And don't you realize that if a man joins himself to a prostitute, he becomes one body with her? For the Scriptures say, "the two are united into one." But the person who is joined to the Lord is one spirit with him. Run from sexual sin! No other sin so dearly affects the body as this one does. For sexual immorality is a sin against your own body. Don't you realize that your body is the temple of the Holy Spirit who lives in you and was given to you by God? You do not belong to yourself, for God bought you with a high price. So, you must honor God with your body."

Ladies, sex is amazing, but wouldn't it be better with your husband? I mean shameless sex!!!! Everyone won't agree, but as for me and my body, we will do it God's way! If you're going to give it away, just be safe, sis! However, you will find more satisfaction if you wait for God to join you with your husband. You are more than just a late midnight snack. You are to be cherished and adored. I know you feel like you've just gotta have it, but the truth is, you are just trying to fill a void. Find out what that void is and allow God to fill it.

Give yourself the grace to turn away from sex before

marriage. Believe that any man who is worth it will be willing to wait. You would be surprised at how many men actually don't mind waiting. Like I said in the previous chapter, we make things so easy for men! Allow God to work in your heart and body. Hold on and wait on God to send you your forever sex partner!

Dear Lord,

We thank you for allowing us to see ourselves as more than a snack. Father, help us to value ourselves more than we have in the past. Allow us to begin to set boundaries in our lives. Allow us to begin to see ourselves as you see us. Allow us to not be careless with our bodies. God, I pray that you allow us to want to wait until we are married to have sex. We pray that you allow us to begin to set boundaries in our intimate lives. God, I ask that you keep us safe from any incurable diseases and out of harm's way. Lord, as we continue to move in the direction you are leading us, keep us encouraged that WAITING IS DOPE! We thank you and bless your name. In Jesus' name we pray! Amen!

FACET
Sixteen

"Who Wants a Microwaved Situationship?"

Just in case you aren't hip to the terminology, a situationship is a false relationship that has no real substance. Nine times out of ten, we dived right in without consulting God. Hold on. I jumped into this topic too quickly! I'm sorry, sis! I got excited and ahead of myself. Let's start over!

Let's start with a little honesty. Have you ever been in a single season and wondered why the Lord was taking so long for your Boaz to find you? Have you looked at those around you and seen how amazingly happy other women seem to be and wondered when it would be your turn? Yes? Girl, me too! Has God told you who your husband was, but he hasn't released either of you to meet each other yet? If you're anything like me, that last question is my life! September 2018, God revealed to me who my husband was. First of all, I was shocked because it wasn't who and what I thought I wanted for my life. The crazy thing is, God highlighted him to me in August of that same year! I remember saying to God, "Okay, and why are you showing me him?" Little did I know, God had a word for me less than a month later.

Now, God knows he can't give me some information like this and not think I wouldn't be ready to walk right into that thing. I wanted to hit the start button, pass "Go," and collect my $200! I was ready for what was next.

Facet Sixteen: Microwaved Situationships

God said, "Child, hold on! It doesn't work like that!" At this point, I'm very confused, like ""Whet?" God, you told me who he was, and now you're telling me I can't have him now? What kind of games are you playing? God, this is not fair!" I have conversations with God like this all the time. I have to be honest with how I'm feeling.

Instantly, God had to remind me of my last situationship. God said, "Because you were so quick to jump into that, it wasn't right, and it didn't work. You took matters into your own hands, and you did not include me. I made it end as quickly as it began. You didn't seek me first, you didn't ask me if he was the one, you didn't ask me who sent him, and you didn't ask me as your Father if he was good enough for you!" WOW! This hit me hard because I never want to disappoint my Father!

When trying to date someone, we have to first ask God if this is something and someone he wants for us. Allow yourself to seek guidance before you push start. What I realized was, because I did not properly allow that situation to develop into a relationship and was in a rush, I ended up with unrealistic expectations that I never set with the person. I guess I felt like that man should have been able to read my mind.

We, as ladies and believers, have to develop a solid foundation with the man God sends us to be helpmates to! The same way God developed everything at the beginning of time. Read Genesis 1 -3 in the Bible if you aren't familiar with this reference. There is a process that we must go through in order to receive the promises of God. There are things that God wants to work through and out of us before he gives us his best. Allow God to work on the things that are not right within you. You want a savory, long-lasting relationship, and not a quick snack that will leave you wanting more. The person you may be dealing with may not know how to satisfy your appetite, so, sis, please don't waste your time! Remember, the goal is marriage and mortgage...not relationship and rent!

Dear Lord,

Thank you for taking me through a process. Thank you for not allowing things to happen like I wanted them to happen. Develop me into the woman you had in mind before the creation of the world. Help me to become the woman that the future generations can look up to and learn from. Remove those things in me that are not like you. You are the ultimate creator of everything, and I submit myself to you that you may do a complete work within me. Just as diamonds take some time to be pressed and polished, I ask that you refine me into the beautiful jewel I am to be in your timing. Even though I may not like the time it takes, I trust your timing, Lord! It's in your name I pray! Amen!

FACET
Seventeen

"What Happens When Your NOW encounters God's NOT YET?"

Before we get started, I want to thank my Pastor for this topic here. During a night of worship in Nashville with our other church campus, God allowed this to be the title of his sermon. I was able to type the title of his sermon into my notes on my phone, but that was it because the atmosphere shifted right after that.

Weeks went by, and God kept having this message to pop up on my phone as a reminder. The first couple of times, I kept ignoring the message. Then, I realized that God was speaking to me. He said, "Adrienne, what do you do when I say, 'not yet'?" This blew my mind because I knew God had some things for me, but I knew they were not manifesting. At this time in my life, I was sitting waiting for my blessings to come to me. I wasn't out here working for them. Because I was waiting, I began getting discouraged and started second-guessing if I heard God correctly, if I heard myself, or did God lie to me? Now, before you start questioning if I called God a liar, we are human, and we do question God from time to time. It's perfectly normal. This is how we learn his will for our lives. That's why the scripture says in Numbers 23:19(ESV), "God is not man, that he should lie, or a son of man, that he should change his mind. Has he said, and will not do it? Or has he spoken, and will he not fulfill it?" Often times, God will give us a word or phrase that we need to address and get clarity on. We tend to want to reap the benefits of the blessings, but never want to do the work. That was a whole message right there for somebody, and I hope you received it!

My question for you ladies is, "What happens when your "now" encounters God's "not yet"?" As much as I didn't want to deal with this and face the facts, it has not been easy to accept this truth! As of September 2019, I've been single AND abstaining from sex for almost four years. This right here is where I insert my praise break! It hasn't been easy because I've been accustomed to doing things my way. God put a mandate on my life, and this was when I realized I wasn't ready to fully submit to his will. I wanted to continue to do things my way, but God said it was time to get serious. I know before God sends me to my next elevation in life, I have to complete and produce some things in my single season. God really wanted me to discover me in this single season and to produce this book. It has been an amazing ride -- once I started to embrace it. There are so many people who see this new "glow" that I have about myself these days. I laugh because it is God that they are seeing! His work is amazing. He will make you like new.

I remember in September 2018, God spoke to me about my life, my future, my husband, and my calling. Let me let you all in on something. This is the first time I've spoken about this with anyone. I've very protective of my personal life. I questioned God because this wasn't the life I chose for myself. I was good with hanging out, traveling, smoking weed, drinking, and having lots of sex. In the middle of my mess, God came to me and said it was time for me to straighten up because I was starting to walk into ministry. After this, I laid on the floor in my closet and cried for an hour straight. Ministry was something I didn't want to do.

As I began to live my "new life," things weren't adding up to what God told me. I even found myself getting frustrated with God. I was like, "This is what you said, and it's not happening! Remember, I didn't ask for this life. This is the life you chose for me!" I was frustrated because my right now wasn't looking like what God said. I wanted to throw in the towel, and God threw it right back at me and said, "Keep going." I even told God I was not doing this assignment. I began to think, "Honey, you have come this far. Where are you going to go?" I began to get mad as hell because I felt like this was a trick and set up. I felt like God had lied to me, and then I read 2 Corinthians 1:20 (NIV) said, "For no matter how many promises God has made, they are "Yes" in Christ. And so, through him, the "Amen" is spoken by us to the glory of God."

After reading this scripture, I resolved to wait until God sent his promises into my life. I know without a doubt that it's going to be better than I can imagine. God also placed James 2:17 (AMP) on my heart. It says, "So too, faith, if it does not have works [to back it up], is by itself dead. [inoperative and ineffective]. In other words, "Faith without works is dead." At that moment, I realized it was time to start producing some things in my life and wait on God to release what's mine when the timing was right. I encourage you to get out and handle your business until God allows you to walk into your destiny.

Father God,

I thank you for not allowing us to settle in our waiting phase. Thank you for making us the creative women we are. Thank you for allowing us to create projects, increase streams of income, establish homes, become entrepreneurs, write books, and any other thing you've created us to do. Father, we ask that you teach us how to be patient in our waiting phase, even though it may not look like what you said. Thank you for helping us to learn more about ourselves during this time. Father, continue to make us into the best version of ourselves. We thank you and love you, Father! It's in your name we pray. Amen!

FACET
Eighteen

"Sis, What Is Your Prayer Life Like?"

I remember when I would give God my good "nursery rhyme" prayers like, "Lord, thank you for waking me up. Thank you for starting me on my way. Thank you for blessing me, protecting my family and friends, and keeping us from dangers seen and unseen. In your name I pray. Amen!"

God said, "Girl, that's cute and all, but I know you have more in you than that!" Don't get me wrong. If this is the way you pray, don't be ashamed. A prayer is meaningful, no matter how short or long it is, so long as it comes from the heart. Baby, pray the way your heart feels led to, and the way your heart desires. Some people get up every day and don't say a word to God. I'm like, "How sway?" This Man gave you another day to breathe, and you say nothing? That breathe you take every 5-6 seconds is because of God's breath within us. Genesis 2:7 (NLT) says, "Then the Lord God formed the man from the dust of the ground. He breathed the breath of life into the man's nostrils, and the man became a living person." So, if you are saying something to the Man upstairs daily, you are doing a lot better than most! However, the purpose of this conversation is to cause you to give some attention to your prayer life, aka your conversations with God.

As for me, I've got to talk to God DAILY! I thought praying every morning was good enough. Then, I went

Facet Eighteen: Your Prayer Life

to every morning and night. Now I have to talk to God multiple times a day. I find myself praying for other people constantly, I ask him for a clearer understanding, I seek strategy for business and relationships, and most importantly, I talk to him about how much I love him. I also thank him for choosing me as his daughter because he didn't have to, but he did.

Even though I asked you what your prayer life was like, I didn't necessarily mean physically praying. Prayer, for you, could be meditation and music. It could be just sitting still listening to God. It could be journaling or worshipping. Whatever it is, don't allow anyone to make you feel like it's inadequate. Trust me, when God wants more from you in prayer, he will make it crystal clear!

Everyone deals with different things. Your desire to pray and sincerity of the prayer depends on your spiritual growth and maturity. Right now, you may only pray for your family and those you love. Eventually, you will learn to pray for your enemies, the world, political issues, pandemics, racism, sexism, peace, and financial freedom. Start small and build yourself. Like with anything else, you have to begin somewhere. The more you pray, the more it will become a habit. Before you know it, you will be running to find a quiet moment in the day to chat with your heavenly Father!

Dear Heavenly Father,

Thank you for keeping me through every test and trial. Thank you for sending your Son to die on the cross so that I may live. Lord, give me the desire to build my prayer life. Give me a hunger to research your word, and write it on the tablets of my heart. Place scriptures on my mind so that I may remember them during prayer. Download in me the areas of focus I should begin to pray about. Right now, I speak life over myself. I bind every evil attack, temptation, doubt, and negative thought and place them at your feet, Father. I ask for peace in my life. Lead and guide me in the direction you see fit. Grant me insight on my purpose. Allow me to love myself unconditionally. Lord, I thank you, and it's in your name I pray. Amen!

Facet Eighteen: Your Prayer Life

Is your prayer life is consistent? Why or why not?

What are some things you could do to strengthen your prayer life?

What are your favorite scriptures?

FACET
Nineteen

"Be A Woman of Faith!"

Let me tell you how strategic God is! So in May 2019, I decided to get a new tattoo. It was random because I'm spontaneous like that. Well, I get this tattoo that represents the heartbeat or cardiac rhythm (for my nursing readers). The beginning of the tattoo is a heart, and the end of the rhythm spells out the word, faith. I got it because 1. I'm a nurse. 2. My life definitely depends on my faith. 3. I walk by faith and not by sight. The tattoo is on my forearm, so I can't see it. "Not by sight." Get it? Anyways, four months after I got this tattoo, our Pastor launched a #GR8FAITH campaign. I'm like, Lord, you are really testing me! The campaign basically challenged us to identify the things we were believing God for and have the faith to see those things manifest.

 I knew, at this point, God was stretching me and my faith. He wanted to see how much I really trusted him and believed that his promises are "yes and amen." God revealed some things to me that year, and I didn't believe him. I was like, "God, stop playing with me!"

 Where my faith started to waver was when things weren't looking like what I thought they should look like. These are the days when I got discouraged and began to cry because I second-guessed God. I heard time after time that God hears your prayers, and he knows the desires of your heart! Let me tell you something. If you're reading this, then that means God answered my prayer in this area of my life. I knew that I was supposed to write a book, but never in a million years did I think that I WOULD WRITE A BOOK! I shared that to let you know that God will never disappoint you. He will stretch you, but never disappoint you! All you have to do is trust him, endure the process, seek him in everything you do, and know that your dreams will definitely become reality if you work hard and follow God's lead.

This is where I want to give you hope. During the #GR8FAITH campaign, we as a church believed God to grant us ownership of our church building. God told our Pastor at the World Changer's Summit in Chicago that there must be a revival to take place at our church. He wanted to see if we as a body would pursue him. Well, we did, and guess what? WE GOT THE KEYS! Because we believed as a whole, God supplied all of our needs according to his riches in Christ Jesus.

God will never have you looking like a fool out here. It may feel like it at times, but he's working in your favor. You'll see it on the other side of your storm. Trust God! Can I pray for your faith?

Lord,

I pray that you would increase the faith level of every woman reading this book. Father, whatever you have told them, whatever dreams they have dreamed, whatever visions you have shown them, and whatever you have placed on their heart, may they believe it and hold fast to it. I pray that each woman does not lose hope. I pray that she presses in harder, holds your hand tighter, and trusts you even more. I pray that if they shall waver in their faith, that they are honest with themselves, acknowledge it, and talk to you about it. According to your word in Luke 8:13 (ESV), "And the ones on the rock are those who, when they hear the word, receive it with joy. But these have no root; they believe for a while, and in time of testing fall away." We ask that they hold on to see what the end will be. Father, send people that will help to keep them encouraged, so they don't have to do this faith walk alone. We thank you for the things that are already ours. We ask for increased faith in all areas of our lives. It's in your name we pray. Amen!

Facet Nineteen: Be A Woman of Faith

What are you believing God for?

How can you increase your faith?

FACET
Twenty

"Encourage Others!"

You can't be around me for more than two minutes without getting some typed of encouragement. This is what I do, and I don't know how to shut it off. I'm so passionate about seeing people being free, saved, and loving life. I push those around me as much as I can. I love that God created me to be an encourager.

On October 4, 2019, I sat in Starbucks and wrote this chapter. Before I began, I reflected over my workday, which was stressful, may I add. It was after 5 pm, so I decided not to give that any energy and, instead, put all of my focus into writing this chapter. As I began to write, I couldn't help but smile. Even though my day was rough, I encouraged people around me all day long. I once heard a great man say, "To live the life of a believer, you have to know you are living an interrupted life!" This is so true.

I wasn't always willing to love on people and encourage them so much. I was actually mean as hell. Hateful, low down, spiteful, and petty, baby! As I reflected on how much I had changed and matured, I was in awe of God. Considering everything I had going on at work, I found time to encourage a coworker I hadn't talked to in a while. A few months prior, she told me about some things she was going through, and I listened and encouraged her to seek God. You do know he is the truth, way, and the light? Well, anyway, I had

Facet Twenty: Encourage Others

seen her at work that day, and she looked AMAZING! She had taken some time to herself, worked on her, and it showed. She told me how her relationship with God had gotten deeper, she was hearing his voice more, and she was getting ready to be baptized! This blew my mind! One seed of encouragement helped her turn her entire life around.

I'm definitely not taking any credit for any of this. This was all of God's doing. It was a part of the plan. He just used me as the vessel. This is huge for me because I realized that I had passed an assignment. I did what God wanted me to do. I planted good seeds, and God allowed me to see some of the fantastic things that were happening in her life. Inserts happy dance here!

When you decide to live for Christ, amazing things begin to happen! There have been times I've poured into people, encouraged people, been a listening ear to people, and have come back home drained. It doesn't take much to encourage people, but you must use discernment for those that may consume you. People will drain you if you let them, but we still have to love as God loves. Use wisdom as you encourage those around you. 1 Thessalonians 5:11 (ESV) says, "Therefore encourage one another and build one another up, just as you are doing." Learn to protect your pour.

As you learn to be more intentional about encouraging others, don't forget to encourage yourself!

As a matter of fact, If no one has told you, I just want to tell you that you are doing a wonderful job, girlfriend! Keep up the great work. It looks very good on you!

God,

I thank you for my sister who is reading this today. Send her the encouragement she needs to keep going. Help us not become afraid of what you have called and created us to be. We thank you that you are constantly pouring into us so that we may pour into others. God, I ask that you heighten our discernment when it comes to those around us that need encouragement. We thank you for the lives that we will change just by being obedient. We ask that you cover them and always protect them. We ask that you send people to pour into us as much as we pour into others. God, we ask for fresh revelations and new downloads daily. We love you, and thank you! Amen!

FACET
Twenty-One

"Be Courageous! You're a Wild Woman!"

Crown Her Diamond

Since I was a little girl, I have loved cheetah and leopard print. I mean, it's everywhere! I wear it often, and it's in my house. I guess you can say I knew I was different and set apart at a very early age. Once I matured, I realized that I am a WILD ONE! I'm spontaneous, strong, courageous, bold, unpredictable, unfiltered, a free spirit, and very protective of those I love! You probably guessed this, but I wasn't always this bold about my personality. Growing up, I was very timid.

Do you remember "The Wiz?" Yes, the more ethnic version of The Wizard of Oz. That's the version I love. I love me some Michael Jackson. Rest on, sir! Okay, so do you remember the cowardly lion? He was afraid of everything. All he wanted was some courage. We all know what happened in the end. He got that thang! Let me tell you something. When I submitted to the will of God, that's when I found my courage. See, the lion went to see the Wizard for his courage, but I went to God! It's only in God can we find the strength and the courage to be who he has called us to be.

Since receiving my courage, I found my place in this world. I found my voice! I no longer second guess my strength, and I definitely won't fall into someone else's weakness!

You, too, are courageous and unimaginably strong. First, you must learn whose you are and then who you are! You are fearfully and wonderfully made. You are the head and not the tail. You are above and not beneath. You have been called. You are the Proverbs 31 woman everyone talks about. All you have to do is believe in yourself! Seek God first, and everything else will follow! Know that God created you with a purpose and a plan. He designed you to be "YOUniquely" you on purpose. Be bold in your authority because God gave it to you! You are the daughter of a King, and you have dominion and power. Don't be afraid to walk in it! Let's Pray!

God,

We thank you for the women you have called us to be. We believe that we are strong and courageous. We walk in the full authority of who you have called us to be. We will never second guess who we are. We will affirm ourselves DAILY even when we don't feel like it! We won't wait for someone else to affirm us. We will never again allow man to tell us who we are. We will appreciate how you made us, and we won't be apologetic for it. We thank you and love you. It's in your mighty name we pray! Amen!

Hey Sis! Repeat these affirmations daily.

1. I AM STRONG
2. I AM COURAGEOUS
3. I AM LOVING
4. I AM KIND
5. I AM BOLD
6. I AM CHOSEN
7. I AM LOYAL
8. I AM BEAUTIFUL
9. I AM SMART
10. I AM LOVED AND BLESSED
11. I AM GOD'S CHOSEN ONE
12. I AM A WIFE
13. I AM A MOTHER
14. I AM AN ENTREPRENEUR
15. I AM WEALTHY
16. I AM HEALTHY
17. I AM WHO GOD CREATED ME TO BE

WORDS FROM THE AUTHOR

First and foremost, I thank God for giving me life and always sending the right people in my life. Whether they are still present, or if their season has ended, I'm grateful for every encounter and lesson. I want to acknowledge my family and friends who have pushed me, encouraged me, cried with me, loved on me, and supported me along the way to completing this book.

I want to say how proud of myself I am! This journey has not been easy, but it has been worth it. I have cried many tears. I've smiled often because I AM AN AUTHOR Y'ALL!

I want to thank my grandmother, Hannah "Madear" Parker (Rest in Paradise, my love), for telling my father to take me because she knew my life would be better with him. I completed writing this book on your birthday. November 13, 2019, will always be a date I cherish. I pray that I have made you, Daddy, Mama, Gran-Gran, and Papa proud of me. I miss y'all so much, and I thank each of you for everything you have instilled in me. This is for us, baby!

The main reason for this book was to help women to see their worth. The things I discussed in this are issues I feel we all go through, but no one talks about them. It's okay. I don't mind being the one who stands out in crowds. I hope I have encouraged multiple women to see the diamond within themselves.

Finally, ladies, keep pushing and keep pressing! In due time, God will polish those rough edges. If I never get the chance to meet you in real life, please know that I love you and wish you the BEST in life! You deserve all of what God wants to give you!

I love you! Thank you for your support and many prayers. Here's to the DIAMOND in you, girlfriend! SHINE ON!

DEDICATION

This book is dedicated to my future daughters and granddaughters. I want you to know that you are beautiful, amazing, strong, courageous, and fearfully & wonderfully made. There is nothing in this world you cannot do once you put your mind to it. Remember that your validation does not come from this world, a man, people, your job, or materialistic things -- it comes from our Father in Heaven.

Psalm 121:1 (KJV) says, "I will lift up mine eyes unto the hills, from whence cometh my help." Seek God in everything you do. There will be times when you think I'm just talking to be talking. You will probably think that I don't know what I'm talking about when I give you advice, wisdom, and insight. Most times, you will probably think I'm trying to take the fun out of the things you want to do. Just know, I, too, have been in your shoes. Know that the things I tell you about life are real because I've once experienced them. I know that I can't protect you from everything, but know I will help enlighten you on a lot of things. I will make sure you are a better woman than I could ever be. You will know how to stand up for yourself, you will be able to articulate your thoughts, you will be able to recognize game when men try to run game on you, you will be able to speak confidently, and you won't be afraid of anything in this world. No matter what, always know you're beautiful, your smile is gorgeous, and you're amazing! Wear your crown proudly. Never knock another woman's crown off -- help her to adjust her crown.

    Believe, my loves, that you are DIAMONDS! I love you dearly, and I'm very proud of the women you will become! Always remember that the sky is the limit. Dream as BIG as you can imagine!

ABOUT THE AUTHOR

Adrienne Figures is originally from Atlanta, GA. She moved to Huntsville, AL with her father at a very young age. She graduated in the top 20 of her class at J.O. Johnson High School. She was involved in Honor's Society, Spanish/Spanish Tutor to local elementary schools, Flag Corp, and so much more. She graduated from Calhoun Community College with an Associates degree in Nursing. Adrienne has worked as a Registered Nurse in different Emergency Rooms, Home Health, Long Term Acute Care Hospitals, Nursing Homes, Travel nursing, and now works from home as a claims nurse. Adrienne has lived in Huntsville, Montgomery, Atlanta, and Nashville. She loves traveling the world, experiencing different cultures, painting, and trying new food!

STAY CONNECTED

Thank you for reading, *Crown Her Diamond*. Adrienne looks forward to connecting with you and keeping you updated on her next releases. Below are a few ways you can connect with the author.

FACEBOOK Adrienne Figures
INSTAGRAM @adriennefigures
WEBSITE www.adriennefigures.com

www.ingramcontent.com/pod-product-compliance
Lightning Source LLC
Chambersburg PA
CBHW020805160426
43192CB00006B/454